A MINGUS LULLABY

Dane Swan

ESSENTIAL POETS SERIES 232

Canada Council **Conseil des Arts**
for the Arts **du Canada**

ONTARIO ARTS COUNCIL
CONSEIL DES ARTS DE L'ONTARIO
an Ontario government agency
un organisme du gouvernement de l'Ontario

Canada

Guernica Editions Inc. acknowledges the support of the Canada Council
for the Arts and the Ontario Arts Council. The Ontario Arts Council
is an agency of the Government of Ontario.

We acknowledge the financial support of the Government of Canada.
Nous reconnaissons l'appui financier du gouvernement du Canada.

A MINGUS LULLABY

Dane Swan

**GUERNICA
EDITIONS**
TORONTO • BUFFALO • LANCASTER (U.K.)
2016

Michael Mirolla, general editor
Cover design, Dominic Laporte
Interior design, David Moratto
Guernica Editions Inc.
1569 Heritage Way, Oakville, (ON), Canada L6M 2Z7
2250 Military Road, Tonawanda, N.Y. 14150-6000 U.S.A.
www.guernicaeditions.com

Distributors:
University of Toronto Press Distribution,
5201 Dufferin Street, Toronto (ON), Canada M3H 5T8
Gazelle Book Services, White Cross Mills, High Town, Lancaster LA1 4XS U.K.

First edition.
Printed in Canada

Legal Deposit — First Quarter
Library of Congress Catalog Card Number: 2015952389
Library and Archives Canada Cataloguing in Publication

Swan, Dane, author
A Mingus lullaby / Dane Swan. -- 1st edition.

(Essential poets series ; 232)
Poems.
Issued in print and electronic formats.
ISBN 978-1-77183-047-8 (paperback).--ISBN 978-1-77183-048-5 (epub).--
ISBN 978-1-77183-049-2 (mobi)

1. Mingus, Charles, 1922-1979--Poetry. I. Title. II. Series: Essential
poets series ; 232

PS8637.W36M56 2015   C811'.6   C2015-906639-5   C2015-906640-9

In loving memory of
Daniel "Blaxxx" Lewis, 1980–2011

Contents

PART ONE: DARK CLOUDS

Epitaph 10 1
Practice 2
Lullaby 3
Smitten 4
Epitaph 9 5
5 Degrees Below 6
How Great Thou Art 12
The Castle 14

PART TWO: A DIFFERENT DESTINATION

Epitaph 4 23
Urban Meditation 24
Hometown 25
Resuscitation 26
Rubber-necks 28
Epitaph 3 30
The one day later 32
Objectors 33
26.06.2010 34
Epitaph 6 37
She Shouldn't Live Here 40
The 'burbs 41
Epitaph 12 42
If roles were reversed 43
A Silent Revolution 45

PART THREE: FLOWERS BOUGHT IN A NIGHTCLUB

Epitaph 1 57
The Blues 59

Entering mid-life 60
Epitaph 8 61
Spadina and Queen 63
The Jazzman 64
Dancehall 66
Grooves in Vinyl 67
Epitaph 11 69
Miracle Worker 70
Epitaph 7 71
To the drunk guy in the elevator last night 72

PART FOUR: THE GOOD LOOKING

Epitaph 2 77
Reincarnation 79
Fear — a work in two voices 80
Stopwatch 84
No(n)Sense 85
Young Yogi 87
A box of Polaroids 88
Left 89
Right 90
Soothsayer 91
Loss 92
Epitaph 5 93
Timbre 94
Epitaph 13 96
Egg Drop and Mushroom Soup 97
Time Travellers 99
The Cedar Tree 100
Epitaph 14 103

Notes 105
Acknowledgements 107
About the Author 109

PART ONE
DARK CLOUDS

Epitaph 10

Who is this? (Dissociative Identity Disorder Part 2)

My man Charles, your autobiography jumps from first person
    to third.

Got me wondering who I am.

Is this Dane or Mingus?
Is this Dane, as Dane, playing Mingus?
Or is this Dane, as Dane in the role of Dane inspired by
    Mingus?
"in resonance with Mingus"
(Or some such)

Said you were three people,
if Dane is playing the role of you,
or is inspired by you,
which version of yourself is he resonating?

Are all three involved?

No, he will not answer your questions until you answer his.

Practice

Turn on the hot water.
Now, the shower head.
Disrobe,
step in.

Soap and lather.
Rinse.
Breathe deeply — begin.

Reach out with your right hand,
smile,
speak.

"Hello, my name is _____.
How are you?"

Remember, smile with your eyes.

Repeat.

"Hello, my name is _____.
How are you?"

Train to be disingenuously genuine.

"Hello, my name is _____.
How are you?"

Shampoo and rinse.

Shut off the water —
don't forget to dry your hair.

Lullaby

Dedicated to John Darrell, Cedar Hill, Bermuda

Dadadadada ... dey, dey, dey .../dey sez I'm a Satan wurshippa,/
cause I don't go ta chuch,/young mens supposed ta blare rock
n roll/or Marley, but I's only play the jazz/on my turntable. I's
only play Mingus,/sing along to Monk, go ta sleep wit'/Ornette
singin' melodies wit' does horns./de white folk tink I'm crazy.
ta dem bass is/played with bow, lykalyka — like a viola/not like
deez genius. Dey genius!/

Ev'ry dey I go ta work, work hawd an honest/Haaawd! Dis wild
jungle muuuzic my release/Mingus knows de madness, Monk
knows da pain/Parker and Buddy hav' nuffin on em! But dey
caan't hear it,/call me Diablo! I don't mine, meens I stay home/
Sunday, tap my toes to "Better Get in Your Soul"/

gess dey scuuured. Cawl de men in da white suits,/tayk me to
da pinkhouse on de hill, da funny fawm,/giv' me a room wit
pillows on da wallz, takeway/mi turntable, hav da priest pray
ova me, tell mi repent!/I do no such ting! 'least ma mine iz
free. 'least deez songs/still wit me.

Smitten

Witness the shakes.
See the largest man
turn docile — a shadow
falling apart,
desperate for that kiss.

This love affair
made her a fool.
This relationship an infinite loop;
debt a prescription for
her illness.

All he wanted was
a peaceful silence,
a muted echo,
the shell
of a past self.

She wanted
to forget,
but this boyfriend
has her calling
iPhones
from parking lots —
crying.

Epitaph 9

The Chill of Death

They can't feel your warm heart through cold hands.
You shouldn't hang out with fate so much.
He only sends chills to bones,
darling. Makes you pale in the dark.
If only the path to heaven was filled with light.
Your soothing smile would challenge the mortals' sun.
Instead, it hides — camouflaged.

You hide — beauty.

If I could steal you, I'd show you
the tragedy of hell — the place where fate
sent me. Misery in all its perfect
lines of symmetry.

I would steal you to heaven. So that you
could breathe a world of imperfect warmth,
and happiness.

Teaching what little I learned of love,
holding your chest against mine.
Chasing chill away.

5 Degrees Below

I

The Earth spun around on its axis,
as it danced its sweet ballet
with the symphony of the Galaxy.
The Milky Way an avid audience;
as they observed, cheered
(only at the appropriate moments in time).
Infinity was crossed thrice.
Time froze 3 times,
twice between movements and scenes,
once for intermission.
All nine planets were impressed by their performances,
their moons gave rave reviews.
However, the mediocrity was better measured
by the results that ensued.

The order created through
chaotic balance was replaced
by archaic order,
designed by low-level math symmetry
rather than high-level math artistry
(which was the design before that day).
Forward evolutionary grace
replaced
by archaic stagnation.
Biological growth overpowered
by technology
Destroying what once neared balance.
All to put structure to a dance —
which received rave reviews

from the honoured few,
who could afford patronage
To witness our Earth, in its dance.

II

Picture this. A poet, legs dangling over the edge of a man-made cliff, elements asleep in a crisp night — 5 below. A breathtaking nightscape. Stars battle streetlights. (The streetlights are winning.) Poet is singing in 5 below, visualizes the world as film.

He imagines

a panoramic view from 35 mm film. Spinning his shivering frame on an imaginary crane. "Now pan back ... yes that's the shot," whispers eyes shut.

The GO Train — a green and white caterpillar, crawls by ... "Greater than whom?" he asks. Drifts into a trance from the mechanical clanging.

boodoomp boodoomp boodoomp boomp boomp boodoomp boodoomp ...

Beside the poet, an old notepad of recycled paper. "It's hard to read without the street lights." Afro littered with pencils, pens. Reaches within the centre of his locks for a ballpoint with jet black ink.

The beat helps him think; he scribes in 5 below.

III

5 below, lower east side Vancouver, her warmth and aura remind you of an old love. Her strength is overpowered by her weakness. Large enough to hold her own — don't feel sorry.

Cold night, 5 below, downstairs from the sky train station just before Stadium in the park, camouflaged by shadows ... she lurks. Desperation has no logic. 2 men walk in the light. "Now I'll get my fix."

She's an old soul who's forgotten her past lives — don't feel pity.

"Give me money." The men try to walk around the 'keeper of the sidewalk' — her reply is a neck thrust. A brutal attack from an old warm soul is the saddest.

One pushes her back, "What do you want?"

"A dollar," she replies, grabbing a fist full of change he tells her to ask politely — "Please!" — she only sees the high 5 minutes from now. Giving her change, the 2 walk on as she disappears — a jaunt to her nirvana.

"Will she remember us?"

IV

5 degrees below 40 Traveller's Corner, Kingston, Jamaica. A beautiful angel invites 5 guests home. Hers a small shack of metal and plastic sheet nailed to a 4 by 4 frame. Her backyard has two oil drums, marked with her name. One full of water to wash, the other, water to drink, cook. Her neighbour has plumbing, she owns a water hose.

One drum is rusty, but she lives the good life. Her man is prestigious in trench towns. No one messes her abode when he's not around. Would tell you she lives the good life. Does hair for money. Her guests sit on tree roots, milk crates she sits behind one on the only chair in the backyard's dirt garden, begins to braid. They chat about 'tings' in different dialects of patois, so many imagination can't decipher. You should see the smile on her.

She doesn't want pity. Demands that she works for her dollar. Speaking of past lives but neither you nor I can understand the Queen's English behind that strong accent.

We smile.

V

It's 5 degrees below, Ottawa — everyone is wearing t-shirts. An old man is suffering from infection, sitting on a park bench. He's dying on Bank Street — don't feel sorry. He has spent the last two years sleeping on that bench, telling jokes for money, cigarettes, whatever.

Police attempt to move him — foreign politicians are coming. Offer him a bed never presented before. Afraid someone will take his place. Can't move; an old chum tells the officer. Officer doesn't understand why he has no health card, radios for aid, thinks.

Witnesses go home and pray, "Dear God, let me hear a bad joke for one more day." In the morrow a compatriot tells them about the man from Nantucket.

Don't feel sorry.

He was loved.

VI

They make the most beautiful number ten.

Her large round hips, his strong slim frame. They hold each other looking out to snow. Forecast says it is 5 below. They were together not long ago, he remembers her kiss as they speak of old times. Her frame does not do her beauty justice; makes the quaint seats in the small coffee place more uncomfortable than they should be.

In their past life they were musicians. Walking in warm nights of their island abode. Accepting each others rough edges .

They smile, circulated by truck drivers and donut essence. He has a mocha mocha something, she has a simple grey tea. She says, "If things were different ..."

VII

"... It ... is ... too cold ... to write ... without gloves ..."

"Picture this," the poet scribbles, "a grin on every man, woman, child."

In this symphony we are mere kids, playing guessing games of whom, what, if. We cannot all play first violin; some of us have to play the triangle, sing.

Peering upwards to see dawn approaching. Cityscape awakens; imagines retreating to a den, yawns. The caterpillar is back. Smiles, shouting, "Maybe another day!"

Frames the sun's rise with thumb, index, "What will the spirits think up next?" The night was only 5 below. Street people greet the world with survival and we have the audacity not to say hello.

Don't feel sorry, say hello.
Don't feel pity, say hello.
Don't feel guilty, say hello.
Say hello,
do what you can —
breathe.

This is an orchestra.

Pick up your instrument, follow ...

It is 5 degrees below.

How Great Thou Art

Wildstyle breaks
monotony.

Obliterates grey
blah, urban sprawl.

Adds colour.
As much an "I was here,"

as an autograph.
A "take a picture it'll last longer."

Temporary masterpieces thrown up
to swiftly be torn down —

more than just a tag,
you're it,

tag,
you're it,

tag.

Caps lie on
metallic heads.

Bleeds are covered,
not bandaged.

Late-night, back-alley ways
become galleries.

Tunnels —
cathedrals.

Crime, holy.

The Castle

I

Eyes shut, darkness.
Eyes ajar, darkness remains,
below, a diamond-hard metal futon frame
sheathed by a crepe thin cushion
falsely called mattress.
More duvet than mattress
"Not like what my mother would call a mattress."
Not the type kids can jump on.
"My princess shall have to be the opposite of fairy tales,
tough,
if she is to move here."

Arms straighten.
Pushing a globe into the abyss
reflecting small flecks of orange as it
ascends, descends with mutated
lines of longitude, latitude
in muted display,
thinking back on the past day,
"Parting is such sweet sorrow."

Outside whispered, screaming popping sounds,
the debate:
Firecrackers, gunshots,
arson, murder?
Fun, or police power?
Dawn radio broadcasts will answer,
but rest beckons, on a diamond-hard futon,
its razor-thin mattress,
eyelids shut within his cell-sized castle.

II

Mattress ... futon ... rodents.
This is a castle not 'the Ritz.'
A hotplate stove,
three feet from king's head.
The throne is down the hallway shared by lords, jesters.
The court's peasants slumber in the foyer.
All asleep, guarding the court.

The guard,
a feeble, homeless addict
affectionately nicknamed Fred.
His cologne essence of urine,
smiles. Lives off tips,
grocery bits, change,
clothing from his clientele.
Once a week he slips in to shower.

III

Existence here is stone soup,
each individual must add their ingredient.
Next door neighbour provides motherly love.
Old, decrepit, blind from cataracts.
God-fearing,
gives the landlord lip for swearing.
Her tiny abode littered with crosses, Madonna idols.
Knits daily, evil comes to hands idle.
Coughing in her yellow stained wall,
dust filled apartment,
she drinks from the same mug.
Once a week the 'king' visits
reads the paper, gives her a hug.

Tomorrow she will not rise.
The members of the court shall circulate.
Waiting
for the moat to fill with tears.
Gods, mortals
honour her existence —
holding their breath.
The land has lost its goddess of love and wisdom.

IV

She is discovered.
The court mourns. Fred hums 'abide with me'
loyal subjects join the chorus.
Grey skies.
Neighbouring pigeons scream harmonies.
This is the Queen Mother's royal wake.
As a young petite female
falls to her knees, wails.
The diminutive girl is the royal cook —
the only person who can make more than Ramen Noodles.
She made meals for her.
Not a soul asks of her past
nor do they believe she's twenty.
Even seventeen-year-old runaways
can trust people they feed.

She works down the street in a rundown
roach-filled, dark dingy diner
with a flickering neon sign
that blinks 'all d_y br_akfa_t'
as a waitress,
but, the court calls her 'little chef'
beg for samples,
the only apartment that
has an attractive aroma —
pine sole, papaya.

V

Downstairs, below the chef, the heart, the king
lives a young family.
Mother, child, numerous 'friends.'
Infant spends more time with the three above.
Has one less person to teach her love.
"You have one less baby sitter today,"
mom says.
"This'll make things tough on busy days."
Little girl thought old lady invented sun rays.
Meanwhile, the couple a door across keep a watchful eye.

Call them all seeing
the royal eyes
or, spies.
Peephole must be ultra — magnified.
Walls must have stethoscopes attached —
knowledge of all is within their grasp,
keep the king up to date with incidental
meetings in the hallway.
Today they pray.
Above them their favourite neighbour passed away,
the building smells of decay.
Wish they could adopt
(the neighbour's child).
Eyes trained on her
future, safety.
They have no shame.
Even if they are perceived as weird,
do not know why they cannot conceive,
do not care. Her safety is more important.
They know the girl cared for the old hag.
Her mother will not let her grieve.

VI

And then there is the 'other' guy.

Obese, heavy breathing
apartment barely large enough
for his king-sized broken bed.
Surprised that she died
before him.
Loses thousands of calories
squeezing in and out of the kingdom,
but her heart's ceasing
gives him determination —
clearing fridge; rubbish bin
bursts at seams.
Talks to his mother in dreams.
She smiles,
at least now he is giving life a try.

VII

The super, grumpy,
stressing, today mourns.
"She hadn't paid her bill in two months,
she must have known the time was near.
I could see her ill health."
They used to shout,
but the last few months, lessened.
Used to slip in, tell her hi.
Her money was not good before she died.
Six feet, balding, plumber's butt.
The executioner,
his door knock garnered fear,
but for a day he sits on a rickety-wood stool in the
basement's work room, silent.

It rains for three days.
The castle places flags at half mast.
The Queen Mother has passed.

PART TWO

A DIFFERENT DESTINATION

Epitaph 4

3 Paths

Louis was owned by Glaser.
Dizzy built a nest egg before saying his piece.
Bird put it all on the line from the git.

There's your choices.
Charles, choose one.
No, you can't pick two, just one.

Parker, and Dizzy are
going to the same place,
but one road is more treacherous.

Try as you may,
you cannot
split yourself in two.

Urban Meditation

All in unison
Her children seek nirvana
Between the red lights

Hometown

Town of empty belly, no identity, abusive culture — civilized. These glass cells we call home. Brick penitentiaries labelled neighbourhoods.

To be alive — live in the middle of everything. Drop etiquette, "Know thy neighbour," barter at markets, hold the heartbeat of a city — action, people — as a cubic zirconia given by a loved one. To feel. Unbridled by trivial niceties. Drop silly walls. (The poor don't want your money; they want their own.)

Laugh in the rain. Cry for good reason. Cry until dehydrated — unable to produce a tear. Take the city's pulse like a naturalist; naked, barefoot.

The oxygenation of a city. This starving beast. Ugly, but she is our child — we think she's beautiful. Melanoma, cataracts must have our eyes. Embrace noise. Prosper within mess. Fucking live for once. Live! Refuse property management propaganda. A condo is not a community. The Universe does not rotate around you, it orbits around our child.

This is our baby,
streets,
home,
city.

Resuscitation

Hands clasp, hand clapping
empty sound, loud but heard by no one
but the sound
sounding off into a blur.
— Garmamie Sideau, "In response to Nina Simone's Sinnerman song."

I balance my heart on the edge of razor blades,
trying not to pierce my aorta
(my heart bleeds).

I'm a black nigga, immigrant nigga, legal problems nigga. I'm
everything I fight; fucking stereotype. Looking for a hot-forty-
year-old, president of a publishing company. Whisk me to your
manor with Raptors TV; shelves stacked: Greek philosophy,
tales of Anansi, old soul records, my favourite spoken word CD
by Garmamie.

(my heart bleeds).

Sick of niggas using the word nigga lightly. Of niggas who think
stupidity is pretty. Got C's in school. Other kids hid comic
books, between text books, I hid my copy of "The Egyptian
Book of the Dead." Failed math studying architecture —
towers from before ancient times in the horn of Africa. Got an
A minus in music 'cause that teacher didn't like me.

(my heart bleeds).

My anger management coach, slowly, surely convinces me.
Couldn't do what I do. Suggests a minor augmentation towards
conformity — we are in a white society. I agree. No more Afro.

(my heart bleeds).

Remembering history class. Covered three tribes of Africa in two weeks — didn't study that other bullshit. Let's guess, crazy dude from one country starts war with another, that is ruled by his sister, cousin, brother. World War One was a family feud. Ever wonder why the West is crazy?

My heart bleeds on "The Razor's Edge." Descendant of slave, and German Jew lynched because of love.

(my heart bleeds).

Where is my forty-year-old goddess? There you are. I'm sick of being another need to be rescued from myself nigga. It's everybody else's fault nigga. Can't do shit for himself nigga. Just one of those niggas. I'm sick of being nigga enough to think that you could save me. Instead of seeking peace; finding myself.

Rubber-necks

(Or somewhere an editor cringes at the repetition of the word "you")

Hey you!
Stop slowing down.

There's nothing to see
here except other drivers

dropping to a crawl,
staring out there

side windows.
You highway rubberneckers.

You believe you are alone.
That's why you slow down.

spoiler alert

You will not die alone.

You will perish surrounded by admirers,
people you cherish,

persons you despise
that are inspired by you.

It'll be okay to laugh —
you will nearly be dead.

They will not stop being affectionate.
The word love will start to make sense.

But you can't see that
ending.

Adding your face to a long line;
shifting your shoulders with

the choreographed precision of
synchronized swimmers.

Each of you hoping it's not
a familiar face.

Smiling as you realize someone's
child couldn't 'hold it in.'

Epitaph 3

Dissociative Identity Disorder

Which one of you is standing in front of me?

Is this the truthsayer or tale-slinger?
Photographer or composer?
English banker or pimp?
Loving father or failed husband?

I like to know who I'm talking to.

In exchange, I'll tell you who I am — eventually.

So who went to Europe,
passed through Detroit,
made San Fran home,
moped in NY?

No,
that one saw Europe,
the other visited Japan,
I lived in Ottawa,
he sleeps depressed in Toronto,
awaiting his awakening.

Which one of you is standing in front of me?

The trombonist, cellist, bass player?
Nigger, cracker, Chinaman?
Ear musician, classically trained composer?
The masterless slave, the free man?
Or is this the juju man?

I won't answer any more of your questions until you answer
   mine.

The one day later

same fate same expectations same destiny same smiles same faces forgetting same selfishness same snobbery same friends same enemies same voice same tragedies same conflicts same story same optical orifices same continents same dreams same nuclear stratagem same nonsensical hate as the same tribe kills the same tribe kills the same tribe same astronomy same excuses same solutions same cowards same supposed allies same motives same frustration same hope same hope same hope same hope

same dream

Objectors

They look like adolescent weaklings.
So fragile you imagine
the bullied bullying them;
their strength — immeasurable.

Could confuse them for children.
More man than us,
have been couriers of imperialism, death,
decided to defend life.

One admits
he ended numerous existences.
Innocent civilians
haunt dreams.

They look like kids
but are men
trying to skip double-dutch
with children.

26.06.2010

I

If violence were the answer
I would be on the front lines —
Molotov cocktail in one hand,
Communist Manifesto the other,
wearing bright pink,
face in full view —
but rocks keep landing
on innocent heads.

Cops harass virtuous people.
Federal agents keep rapping
on civilian doors. Riot police
should only arrest those rampaging.

Masochists
call themselves anarchists,
in a selfish society
where we protest
mediocre lives.
Violence isn't anarchy;
it's organized failure.
None of this will lead to change.

The only way?
Buy a lobbyist.
If poor people band together
we can change one law —
so which?
If we gave everything
to amend a law,
would we have the courage to give
our crumbs away?
Would what we change,
only serve vanity?

Few vote.
How dare our complacency
we watch people die:
Tortured because they fight
for what we take for granted
from the comfort of our quaint
abodes with digital signal televisions.

My neon pink ensemble
still tucked in a quiet space.
The only bottles were
emptied in revelry. My Communist
Manifesto has gone missing.
No passionate movement
to fight; this is not the solution —
it's just another distraction.
Questions are not being taken seriously.

II

A protest of 30,000
destroyed by 200
with violent intent.

Or was it the 1100 arrests?

Public transit workers, homeless,
couples dating, an amputee —
didn't move fast enough.

Was the law ignoring the rule of law?

Herding innocent like cattle:
40 per cage,
10 by 12 by 10.

Like watching an infomercial,
the same six images
keep repeating themselves
on TV as journalists report
that the city's on fire.

From my high-rise apartment
I can't see smoke.

Epitaph 6

3

I am 3.
Father,
son,
holy spirit.

Man,
child, and
wandering ghost.

Emotionless observer,
passionate lover,
manic loose cannon.

Trapped within a single vessel.

We are conjoined triplets, sharing a single husk. Flailing in attempts for independence, while our motor skills begin their gentle voyage. This body obsolete. Our only passion — music.

Keeps pulling us back. Can't stave it off with photography. Women get in the way, bear offspring, get tired of our good habits. Leaving us alone with sheets of manuscript paper. Two of us hum: melody, harmony, third writes it down. Only thing we agree on.

I am 3.
Father,
son,
holy spirit.

Man,
child, and
wandering ghost.

Emotionless observer,
passionate lover,
manic loose cannon.

Though music greeted our souls at birth, we couldn't read her until adolescence. Felt like realizing she lied about her name years into the relationship. Got us curious to find the truth. Asking outlandish questions to civilized peoples. The path to knowledge is filled with embarrassment, humility, hard work. We each chose one of these burdens.

I am 3.
Father,
son,
holy spirit.

Man,
child, and
wandering ghost.

Emotionless observer,
passionate lover,
manic loose cannon.

One day we shall mature, grow beyond this physical realm of sin. Peel our skin; a cold-blooded creature's growth spurt. Leave these sonic notations behind to prove that this go round was real to the other sisters and brothers who have reached enlightenment. The drugs were really drugs, women really women, but the breakdowns were just breaks in momentum. We could see them comin'. Like how we will see it all slowly shuttin' down.

Children, ex-wives, our lovers will see it comin'. Forgive our transgressions. See us for who we are. Kiss our forehead. Tell us that we are loved. We will reciprocate.

She Shouldn't Live Here

Her neighbourhood, so dangerous
the guard lets strangers in,
gambling if you knew better
you wouldn't wait outside.

She shouldn't live here.

After two hours of
broken elevator,
scary hallway,
dingy apartment with busted furniture,
mattress on floor,
milk-crate seats,
cheap beer libations;
our sweet angel disappears
to sleep it off on the floor
of a cold, tiled, unlit room.
We leave her, her housewarming.

The 'burbs

No hope for unexpected meetings,
every eating place franchised —
a social wasteland.

Happily ever rarely
visits a resting place
never called home.

Dreams died long ago,
now vessels that cogged the machine
haunt cupboard homes.

Lab-mice scurrying for cheese,
sleeping in sterile cages —
accepting inhumanity.

Wake up, drive to work.
Drive home, watch TV.
Turn off TV, go to bed.

Epitaph 12

The Complete City Hall Concert

recording is incomplete.
So was the concert.
Gave the suite a morbid name —
Epitaph; threw a life's work in.

Maybe Fate killed the concert.
waited for your passing to
allow the work to be performed.
She defeated you.
Or, did she?

The complete incomplete session.

If roles were reversed

English was beaten out of your descendants long ago.
You can speak three languages but not that one,
or any other dead language.

We call you anglhost children —
not quite strong enough to be considered human.
Your descendants lost a war,
or, were sold by their parents for food,
or, were ambushed while travelling.

No one really knows,
was around to remember,
cares enough to research how
you were herded like goat.

Your glare is the Devil's glare, your smile — the hyena
     salivating.
The women who love you are thought to be loose.
Your women — objects thrown away.

Pale boy, your smile hides the
frustration of disenfranchisement.

Your children have been free
for two centuries, yet
do not know freedom.

You only have one wife.
We are disgusted that you only have one god,
giggle when the sun god makes your skin burn.
Even I can't help but point when you dance,
such unusual posture — no sense of rhythm.

You are a creature born of shame.
It is illegal for you to not conform.
Yet, your brothers defiantly listen to faulty instincts.
our prisons filled with your resistors.

Brother,
they say that your ancestors were powerful people.
But now, you spectres infest our slums,
steal and sell drugs. After we gave you
the privilege to be free —
this is your apparition.

What little culture your spirit remembers,
we manipulate for currency.
Imitate, simplify, re-express, codify.
Your art, music, dance, literature made
digestible for masses.

You tell one another that, "white is beautiful."
Gained the vote but do not take democracy seriously.
Act as if we are the enemy when we are merely
showing you how freedom is to be grasped — subserviently.

A Silent Revolution

In memory of Qashoush

I.

I woke up, realized
my whisper was more
powerful than my scream.

Screaming made me appear
crazy, or like a
stage actor — but this is no act,

no cry from a lost mind.
These words
personify immediacy.

I don't remember the day.
Was I behind bars,
or a time signature?

Beats assaulted my mind.

These words have power.
Can rustle an uprising.
Be recited in protest —

galvanize masses.
But only when whispered.
Let me appear mute,

so wondering ears are forced
to gather. Quietly becoming
more than just words.

II.

(i)

False rebellion has culling herds docile with fear —
investigating the epidermis of neighbours —
searching for a nesting place to lay blame;

has grown men burning maroon costumes of play;

has William Wilberforce falling in despair
as infant super heroes wear the face of failed treason.

I could have sworn it was November the fifth.

(ii)

Yesterday crime was surviving.

Today we are convicted for rejecting disrespectful symbols of
   our plight.

Tomorrow we shall plead guilty to existing,
laughing in hysterics — we are rejected from our flock.
Witness their freedom to gather in slaughterhouses
from the outside looking in; swearing the North wind tickled
our ear lobes with tastes of November.

(iii)

suckers cant count for shit
they dig shallow graves in gravel
using thirdrate engineered tools of mass production

suckers cant do math
fail to see the correlation between numbers and freedom
when there are only 2 digits to memorize

they giggle at the site of an abacus
circle the cleansing flame
from the wrong side
cause they cant count steps

suckers recount the past as it passes the present

and every year is 12 months of november

(iv)

How brave. Run to the bosom of heaven. Leave your family to
bare arms without your strength. The heroism of burning stars
from continent's divide — lauded. Stripes of his dress-shirt peel
into black-grey. Little ones brainwashed with dancing flames,
cotton candy, sparklers, soda-pop, fireworks. Arms have out-
grown Winter coats. Wrists are exposed to the chill.

III.

What follows you?
Have labels pinned to your
breast sculpted you, made you
submit to subservience, become
a child of fear — a shadow's frail shell?
What is your scarlet letter?
Your metal of shame? The carcass of a pregnant
albatross chained to your malnourished frame?

From freedom fighter to terrorist,
gossiper to journalist;
different sides to
a corroding penny.

IV.

When we were smaller the sky was near.
On tippy-toes we let blue pass
through infant digits.

The sun tasted of strawberry smiles.
Funny faces on TV with grease stained hair
crowed words of importance; that were not.

Being held by a smiling face meant more.
Kissing wrinkled VapoRub cheeks had value —
painted clowns had none.

Today the sky is miles away.
Partners within arm's length
marathon distant.

Cheeks perfect for small
kisses rest below us,
we fear screaming mimes.

The world feels different
to our eyes. But the sun still tastes
like strawberry smiles.

V.

Called many things.

Most negative.

Heroes have become skyscrapers,
barriers,
names to despise.
Burning prophets' bibles
we light a hidden path.

Shall never be gods.
Our crowns bow
to the wilderness,
kiss gales —
sprout in fallow land.

Growing our kingdoms
in poisoned fields;
the circling vultures
exhausted — fly at
eye level.

Basement born opiates the lone elevators.

Despite peasantry,
simpleton garb,
backwards world
of moonshine,
our voices rise.

VI.

There will be no reason to write —
to place pen to paper.
Conflict hushed into
quarrelling corners —
war a forgotten verb.

Justice replaced
with the newest truth.
Docile subservience abound.
Society sterile.
Artist voice muted.

Freedom replaced with equality —
voices eschewed into crawlspaces.
Emotions castrated — the long
kiss forgotten.

VII.

Introduce your voice.
Sing.
Sing loudly,
badly.
With perfect pitch, intonation.
Embarrass your children with your singing,
parents with off-key vocals.
Roar from mountaintop.
Become a superstar at a
dive bar with your karaoke.
The subway platform is a stage.
So is the town square,
the sidewalk, anywhere.
Let the blues warm you.
Hum gospel in the shower.
Metal at bus stops.
Whistle that favourite country
tune while you commute.
Onlookers are part of the chorus.
Lift your voice.
Sing.

VIII.

Become admired by adversaries and compatriots — more than
   a rally cry.

Only a few have potential, a portion shall grab the gauntlet,
   less shall be.

This is not aimlessly following a crowd of untrained mimes.

Sometimes, a march is led by those who walk behind.

A band leader cannot play all of the instruments all the time.
They need skilled musicians, willing to follow to create the
   perfect sound.

IX.

These words
were not born in a safe space.

They commiserate
with embers from the fiercest flame,

suckled
the breast of tainted milk,

gleefully
played amongst lions and sharks,

became
Gulliver in a shrinking world.

The song of huddled masses
gives strength in weakened times.

Far away from docile lands,
hear their echoes within the eye of the storm.

Accepting future repercussions:
This rally's cry.

X.

We must be stupid.

We are honest when the smart are deceitful,
brave when cowardice is logical,
believers when doubters appear clairvoyant.
Maybe, it's because we don't believe in God,
because we do believe in God, because
we believe our messiah can turn oil to wine,
be saved by a spider's web,
our spiritual leader has reached enlightenment.

We believe in truth — a fatal flaw.
In kindergarten classmates stuck
crayons in their ears.
We listened when teacher said to be honest.

We must be naïve — sucker enough to dream.
Others call us inspiring.
See our behaviour as integrity,
carrying larger expectations than we deserve —
using words like great.

As if we had a choice — we are fools.

PART THREE
FLOWERS BOUGHT IN A NIGHTCLUB

Epitaph 1

Monterey Jazz Festival 1965 vs Joshua Chapter 6

God needed seven days of seven priests playing seven horns circling the city of Jericho thirteen times to make the city walls tumble. All I need is one turntable, with one fresh stylus, and one mint-conditioned copy of "Meditations for Inner Peace."

She needed priests, with seven horns, and seven days to do what Charles got Lonnie to do in one: Create a sermon with his horn. Become rabbi, and pastor. Turn the masses into a congregation. Lead them to conviction. Raise them with the spirit. Hold them to the course. Have them bursting at the seams. Wishing to: "Testify!" Shake they souls! Make walls fall!

There was no Holy Arch of the Covenant in Monterey — just an upright double bass, that sang the angelic lullaby of a cello as our worship's introduction; a sonic miracle birthed from Mingus's hands.

In her wisdom only the relatives of Rahab the harlot were allowed to live. In his wisdom Mingus became a pimp — everyone at Monterey was allowed to live. Apostle Charles was demolishing a different set of walls.

She had Joshua order silence amongst her followers for seven days before they wailed her soul-filled cry. Seven days after Monterey, the media still were screaming of his arrival. Not for a second his presence muted.

Hallelujah! Hallowed be thy pizzicato strum.

Praise the Lord!

Preach to me Lonnie!

Testify!

Call me blasphemous. Maybe it's because Ginsberg married him to his fifth wife, because this half black, quarter Chinese, quarter Swedish man defied the term race, yet labelled himself a "yellar nigger," saw himself lower than the underdog, but still found a way to triumph that I am here. Worshipping. Praising his name.

Amen.

The Blues

There will always be the blues —
heartbreak.

Big mama's been done wrong.

A wandering man leaves.

Another guitar needs tuning,
a stage,
patrons.

Entering mid-life

At twenty-five he reached his
mid-life crisis; A woman
two decades senior.

In dimly lit, half-filled lounges,
late-night street cars,
their fingers entwine.

She giggles shyly into
cupped hands after
he tells her his age.

Worships:
her crevices are pews,
mind the sermon.

Each dawn a terror —
praying she never
whispers goodbye.

Epitaph 8

Eclipse

It's fate.

Two celestial beings collide.
Darkness envelops the earth,
solar, lunar congregate.

Sometimes the devil plays fate,
urges the wind to befriend
the travelin' man,
temp him with the many moons of Jupiter —
leave Thebe for Callisto,
absorb the wrath of Hera.

It's fate.

Like the winding road that
formed this chance encounter —
observing eyes mesmerized
by this rare occurrence —
rush for tinted glasses to guard
inquisitive eyes.
Inevitability passes these
corridors only in moments of
sheer happenstance, and convenience.

It's fate.

So why are we observing?
Shouldn't we shrug our
shoulders, walk on
cognisant that this moment
was pre-ordained?

But the Sun doesn't care,
and the moon has no fear.
For destiny is making her choice.

Spadina and Queen

Missing chaos.

Across the way he stood,
in his twenty-year-old
brown tweed
Sunday's best suit.
Standing five-feet-nothing in
scarred, polished black loafers
rescuing masses with: holy water,
touch, a quaint-petite-obedient wife.

"God forgives your sins."
"Jesus loves you!"
"Will you let us bless you?"

Four lanes away.
The bright light shone over them was blocked.

A broken milk crate chair.
A urine stain on the Indian red.

The corporate fast food joint's
washroom permanently an inch
under water — it seemed.

The unique smell of hotdog stands and beer
touching each passerby
on a corner owned by big business.

The same corporations inhabit 3 corners,
but no more baptisms on the way to debauchery,
red brick now shimmering glass,
fast food washrooms hygienic.

The Jazzman

The old jazzman sits in a corner
humming tunes of joy in misery.
Typically his melodies are
temporarily euphoric to fans.
His job: Ease the choke hold
of society, smile.
Musicology students, fans admire.
Never expected fame, smiles to those who
he's seen again, and again. Those
that know his riffs better than he does.
Feels a unique buzz hover
over the crowd when he touches stage.
That's why they leave him alone in his corner,
he reads the local news page,
receives drinks from admirers, thinks of simpler days.

Old jazz man considers music life.
Smiles as he remembers his kids,
lights, stage. But now,
settles for master classes,
gigs at local spots —
locals complain foreigners come
to old man's shows too much.

Jazz man checks his watch,
glances to the next table, tells them,
"Warm up."
Reaches for his horn perched,
makes sure the third valve isn't stuck.

Moment of silence for those who came before.
Master of ceremonies tells the crowd to cheer.
A prayer for three ex-wives,
kids, friends.
His band starts.
Delicately standing up under his own power
(Witness his shuffle to the stage).

Dancehall

I miss the bass,
the wining,
grinding,
and grinding,
warm breasts pressed against
my adolescent chest —
melodies of youth.

We sang along
to an English I rarely hear —
replaced by poor mimicry:
the fantasy of minds
who've never
seen the Atlantic.

Rarely smoked;
always carried a lighter —
anxious for the moment our host
asked us to illuminate the sky.

When I hear these riddims
I feel close to home —
enraptured by passion,
familiar voices
call me.

Grooves in vinyl

These are not age lines. They're more like grooves in vinyl; where dust makes music skip a beat. You could call this failure if it wasn't for the many whose fate was similar. Like marionettes with rotting string our movements are erratic on the lucky days when nothing breaks. But, something is always in disrepair.

In our minds, this is the rebuild after nuclear apocalypse; building makeshift villages within dilapidated iron frames, where towers poked the belly of god. I guess she got angry. All that's left are these hard black that have me scouring for a direct-drive turntable.

When in love, the first thing the musician explains to their lover is rhythm:

"This song is alive. The beat represents the pulse of this living creature. She is a jealous beast. She reflects the soul of her parents. She does not lie. Her honesty is a weapon used to manipulate. Don't look directly in her eyes or you will be a slave to her whims and follies just like the rest of us."

These dark black lines. We are the result of falling down. Punchlines to jokes at our expense. The angst of Emo without all that emotion. Like cutters our last grooves are often silent.

These dark black lines have more in common with black eyes than black skies. They are not the carrier of water to wash it all away — more like a scar of abuse that fades away leaving a permanent memory.

These dark black lines. If you kiss them you will hear the sirens' melody. Will be caught too deep. Searching the coast for a Black Star Liner, but your ship of repatriation is leagues beneath the sea.

These dark black lines are not the result of closed bedroom doors. They swing like ropes on trees. Scared like the horses spooked, running away. Praying to god like the ones of us who remain as bed sheets flutter in the summer breeze.

These dark black lines are like a tattoo. To some, they are the mark of savagery. But to the discerning eye they are beauty telling a personal story to the world like, "I got this one when the person I love threw me away. It marks my freedom."

These dark black lines are grooves that pray for a place to call home imprinted in braille a thousand times. You can call them cliché, or the birthmark of a martyr who never planned to die. Sometimes the choice is made for you. The music writes itself. You get caught in a dark black line and can't pick up the needle. The days keep repeating themselves, repeating themselves and can't pick up the needle.

Look at yourself in the mirror, and wonder if anyone will ever love someone with so many dark black lines etched into their skin. As if love resolves problems. It doesn't. Love makes you feel at peace while surrounded by turmoil. It replaces sleepless nights with comfort, but if it disappears another dark black line appears in the mirror like the voodoo curse that follows my existence.

These dark black lines are more than a metaphor. They are the rings of a thousand-year-old tree reverberating with sonic resonance. They echo life into existence. They are a call to freedom.

Epitaph 11

Freedom

There's no freedom for me

just humiliation. Walking through Watts half naked, pants stolen while skinny dipping. The only hope is a comfortable slavery. Fantasies of paying bills in a timely manner. Slip away to ghost town Saskatchewan, or the Maritimes. Find a little Miss a drive away. Disconnect from the grid. Stockpile bulk foods like a fanatic doomsday militia.

There's no freedom for me

just labour. Sweat, and tears where fantasies once grew. Foreign wild weeds of conformity strangle my wilderness. We trek. Thumb in the sky, avoided like leprosy-infected children. Fisticuffs with failure, conformity. Hope blindfolded, swinging wildly. Be careful, she may accidentally knock you down, confusing your voice for misery.

There's no freedom for

children with dreams beyond terabytes. Men with earth songs, and moon dreams. Women disinterested in soap opera melodies. People submerged in the muck of their lordships, and masters.

So stand fast, young Romeo
stand fast.

Miracle Worker

listen
no
feel

The pulsation

the power from the sub-woofers
kisses from tweeters
energy from our three hundred friends
possessed by ecstatic movement

it's not the thing we took when we got here

open your eyes

binary code in fluorescent green floating
exploding on impact
with dancing bodies

beyond gyrations
waving hands
strobing lights
smoke
laser shows
the dj creates miracles
mutating distortion
glitches
blips
      pops
into organic orchestrations
giving technology

soul

Epitaph 7

Irony

You've been falling in love since little Hoacha held your hand, making fools pay the women you love for love, trying to be true to love when — honestly — you're mistaken. Confused turmoil for love, anguish for beauty, success for hardship, kicked loyal dogs away, pulled vipers to your chest.

I get it. You're an artist. I once stood at the exact same place. Take my hand. At your darkest hour I shall not be light. Just a person holding your hand. Opposite of everything you think you need. Imagine me dark, voluptuous, I'll become pale, slim. Push me away, I'll become your shadow. Yearn for LA, I'll take you to San Francisco. Elope with San Fran, I shall take you back to New York. Try to be misunderstood, I'll become your interpreter. Manifesting myself as everything you don't want, so when you yearn for me you'll realize what love is.

That's what it comes down to. Fats shouldn't have to say. They let you walk away, afraid to hold you back. I refuse to leave, pulling you along the path. I carry your girth, letting go at the Ganges. Only then shall I let go of your hand.

To the drunk guy in the elevator last night

"That's not poetry, it's rap."

How it felt:

You might as well have said, "Go back to where you came from."

As if my blood-lines had not seeped into Western soil generations before yours left tyranny in Europe. I am of the generation of generations of generations. This O positive runs deep through these rocks as much as it flows in the land of my ancestor's ancestors.

This is what it is to be black.

What I wanted to say:

My great great great grandparents were lynched on a tree just like this one.

My great great great great grandmother on the other side was sold on a harbour that looks eerily like this one.

My family has been working fields longer than ghosts can remember — reading in secret just as long. I am not your fool.

What I should have said:

"I'll take the next elevator."

"No this jacket means a lot to me. Don't touch it."
"Good for you. Nice Job."
"If you want to hear my poetry, buy my book."
"Of course it sounds like rap. What do you think rap is?"
"I'm not a monkey for your fucked up amusement."

What I said:

"Sure."
"You want to hear a poem? Sure."
"That is poetry."

PART FOUR
THE GOOD LOOKING

Epitaph 2

Rules of Engagement

Rule # 1

If you are, or are not a black man, but are identified as being black by white society, proceed with caution if you decide to live in an affluent white neighbourhood.

Rule # 2

If you are, or are not a black man, but are identified as being black by white society, and decide to live in an affluent white neighbourhood do not stockpile artillery with plans to become a vigilante, or a one negro-man militia.

Rule # 3

If you are, or are not a black man, but are identified as being black by white society, and decide to live in an affluent white neighbourhood, while stockpiling artillery with plans to become a vigilante, or a one negro-man militia keep said stockpile of weapons, and ammunition a secret.

Rule # 4

If you are, or are not a black man, but are identified as being black by white society, and decide to live in an affluent white neighbourhood, while stockpiling artillery with plans to become a vigilante, or a one negro-man militia, and refuse to not keep said stockpile of weapons, and ammunition a secret do not fire said weapons inside your apartment because your affluent white neighbours are getting you evicted for stockpiling artillery with plans to become a vigilante, or a one negro-man militia.

Rule # 5

If you are, or are not a black man, but are identified as being black by white society, and decide to live in an affluent white neighbourhood, while stockpiling artillery with plans to become a vigilante, or a one negro-man militia, and refuse to not keep said stockpile of weapons, and ammunition a secret, firing said weapons inside your apartment because your affluent white neighbours are getting you evicted for stockpiling artillery with plans to become a vigilante, or a one negro-man militia do not fire said weapons in front of a documentary film crew on camera.

Rule # 6

If you are, or are not a black man, but are identified as being black by white society, and decide to live in an affluent white neighbourhood, while stockpiling artillery with plans to become a vigilante, or a one negro-man militia, and decide to not keep said stockpile of weapons, and ammunition a secret, firing said weapons inside your apartment because your affluent white neighbours are getting you evicted for stockpiling artillery with plans to become a vigilante, or a one negro-man militia, doing so in front of a documentary film camera call your blonde haired, blue-eyed partner to pick you, and your belongings up from the sidewalk so that she can take you to the neighbour-hood she could afford to live in — a couple blocks from the local Black Panther chapter. Expect to never hear the end of the coming lecture about your choice of neighbourhoods. You wouldn't need to stockpile weapons if you lived where you feel at home.

Reincarnation

In a past life this suburb was a city.

The billboards at the train station
welcomed tourists instead of suggesting
that, "You would be home now
if you worked here."

Long drives were vacations not traffic jams.
Kids walked both ways uphill to school.
Now ghost whispers are a cool breeze.

People still live here, but no one lives here.

Fear — a work in two voices

... utilize the past only to help the future,
not as a razor strop for guilts and fears ...

— Charles Mingus, Beneath the Underdog

VOICE 1:

I wish I lived in Peace.
Told my secrets to fauna,
meditated with flora and pixie dust,
beat-boxed concertos to mother nature,
while birds smiled in front of my camera —
I wish I lived with Peace,
instead, I live in —

I know I am, but what are you?

VOICE 2:

(Instructions for Black men who are interested in bird watching.)

While walking to the park at 5 AM do not appear intimidated by the police officer who drives by you, slowing down multiple times. He's trying to figure out what sort of Black pedestrian is smiling at 5 AM in the morning. If he gets out of his car you're screwed. No cop will ever believe that a Black man would be walking to a park to bird watch. If he uses his baton protect your camera. Police brutality is not covered by your camera's warranty.

VOICE 1:

If it wasn't for decorum
(and laws) my Hell-O'-Weens
would be a play on irony.
Assaulting Black-faced White people,
While wearing Blackface,
screaming, "Black on Black crime!"

Or eschew irony, wear a white hood
and call them nigger right before I attack.
Watch the glint of innocence
in their eyes fade —
reliving my acts of tyranny on tear-filled pillows.

I know I am, but what are you?

VOICE 2:

(Banking while Black.)

I don't have this problem being poor, but if you are Black, or are often mistaken for being Black and you live in Toronto, it is highly likely that you will be interrogated by a teller, have a hold put on your account, or be asked to speak to a police officer for simply being responsible and saving your money.

Since you're Black and you have savings, you might be a drug dealer — forget the fact that most drug dealers make around $20,000 a year. The teller does not care about your business and/ or academic acuity, or, your struggle to be more than a stereotype.

Know your rights. If they want to call a cop, you want to call your lawyer. Close your account. Contact media. Put your money in multiple banks, or use a credit union. It appears that the policy to suspect Black people with savings is not individual tellers being racist — it's policy. Sort of like how ushers at Blue Jays games constantly ask people of colour for their tickets but White people can sit anywhere —

VOICE 1:

I may wish for peace, but don't need it.
I need my resume to have the same value
after you see my face as it did before.
To have a job I'm not overqualified for.
Have the same menial complaints about
my crumby employment as everyone else.

I want to practice my beat-box in the shower instead of
practicing a fake smile.
Be able to tell a police officer,
"I'm going down to High Park to watch birds,"
and be believed.

Have you ever gone to a park at 5 in the morning?
You'll learn whose land this actually is
as wildlife bombard your eardrums
with a racket that says, "You are a guest."

Are you asleep while there's a lesson to learn?
Snakes and critters to observe before
the first florescent-Lycra-clad invader disturbs our peace
wondering why there's a Black man with a camera.
Slowing down, observing as I prepare a pen
for her closeup. Pleased to share a Swan's
first smile with the world.

But the lady in obnoxiously
loud fitness gear just sees a Black man,
and a camera and is —

I know I am, but what are you?
I know I am, but what are you?
I know I am, but what are you?

I know I am,
                but what are you?

Stopwatch

Don't tell me.
I understand the gravity of words.
The weight of your past.
Boulders you carry.
Call me friend. Brush my arm subtly.
Take things slow. There's time to spare —

on walks,
in the wilderness we find a chorus.
Constellations, satellites set the scene.
This hallowed moment,
each second discovering a new excuse to drag feet.

I will give you a timepiece with broken arms.
... it cost me everything.

Time isn't going anywhere.
Neither am I.

No(n)Sense

In resonance with Minimal (Alastair Thompson)

In the first dimension I was but a line. Straight. There was only one path. Peacefully, we congregated at the point of infinity. There were no arguments because there was no choice. Just stark, charcoal greys — we ran over one another.

In the second, I was a painting inspired by anger. The laws of refraction stole colour away. I was pastels, oil reflecting the absence and presence of light. Your still life stared back at me.

In this third dimension. I am just a figment of imagination. A ball of sensory overload. A pattern of mathematics and chemistry smashed together by coincidence. My sharp edges cut. Or do they? Is the piercing of pain authentic or the fictional happening of a non-existent concoction of electron, proton, neutron.

The weight of this conceptualization of reality is killing me in another astral plain.

I am the jagged edge of the serrated knife. The transplanted tree that yearns to return home. The wind- torn sail that rots at the end of the fisherman's dock — never to go back out to sea.

Feel this. The weight of the walls collapsing in. In theory, you could hold them up with a look. You could kill a person with a dirty look. You could even solve the Earth's ills with meditation — your inner look. In theory, but that theory involves comic books — imagination. And I don't have enough change to buy comic books — reality. Plus, feeling is an irrational concept. Our lovers feel no guilt when they seek pleasure in our arms instead of being faithful to their partners' because feelings never made sense.

Feel this. The rugged texture of stone on skin. The impact of sub-woofer speakers pressed against your chest as the DJ turns the sound system up to its maximum. There's nothing to fear on the outer edge of the cliff. We never did feel. We only perceive that we do. If we fall we can return to the simple existence we had in the first dimension.

Do you dream of the days when you were a simple line? And if we were a simple line, would you dream in more than three dimensions?

I dream that I would dream in 4, in 6, in 7 ... as mutated steel pan drums play symphonic melodies. In the 10th I would finally find love — home. She would draw a map to her Cartesian coordinate using the electric synapses of my brain function; implant the thought that I should seek her out when I awake in the 1st dimension. I would run straight into her.

If only I was a simple line.

Young Yogi

She reaches to the heavens —
arching linked vertebrae,
lips kissing sun,
clenched grinning eyes,
open-mouth smile,
with nine gaping toddler teeth.

Her arms reach vertically,
hands spread open —
feeling breeze from
passing traffic.
Her voice sings a song
to urban dwelling songbirds
who proclaim this intersection
as theirs.

Her mother, size six,
five hundred-dollar seaweed blend
high-end yoga wear
says, "Shut up."
Unable to grasp
her daughter's wisdom.

A box of Polaroids

Excuse me,
I'm looking for that box full of those 'other' pictures.
Ones where no one smiles,
show are faults, tears.
Were you not there?
All I can find are swimsuit shots,
Polaroids of glasses raised.

Where are the boxes of mementos from big fights?
Crates full of broken glasses, plates.
Tapes of shrill screams, barked yelling in the nights.
I want to find those boxes.

Between peaks, valleys,
the darkest hours, fantastical highs —
check the bed. I'll mine the closet.
Somewhere there's a realistic photograph.

Hopefully, I can build this,
a connect the dots picture
linking dot to real instances.
Saving those seconds,
cherishing minutes,
appreciating, simple hours.

Left

The crush of the bus pushes me unwillingly towards you. Seated, you feign sleep. I pretend not to know who you are, fail my performance, bend over your frame, press my forehead against yours, kiss. Your chin wrinkles up the same way I remember it.

Words fall from my lips.

I'm sorry for being such a loser.

Each sentence leaves me; plants itself beneath your ribcage,

Everything was my fault.

growing beyond tremors,

It's my fault you cheated on me.

become sobs that shake your chest,

If I was a better man you wouldn't of had to run to other men.

sprouting withered buds.

Faces fill with tears, mucus covers lips. Wrapping your left arm around my neck, your hand pulls me in. Years after the damage, surrounded by tempered chaos — listening. Not to gossiping teenagers, complaining seniors, pre-recorded messages telling patrons to move back, but to our crying. Near my stop I turn around, see my wife's hand stretching through the mess of commuters. My left grasps hers, I awake.

Right

If this was a soap opera
no one would believe the plot.

Invited another man to our first date,
withheld your home number
passing it to strangers
while relegating me to Facebook,
then your cell,
relenting unceremoniously —
saying something about brain tumours.

Two weeks in I thought,
"So this is what love is."
Calmly seeing the fuzzy remnants
of a beautiful image
through the muddled mess.
Patiently accepting petty bullshit.

Half a decade later it's just you, me,
your cat crying for attention,
watching random reality TV.
No other men here to protect you —
gave me a key years ago.
You tell me it was love at first sight.

Soothsayer

I am the result of my flaws
mistakes,
failures,
losses.
Yet treated like a snob,
judged ornery,
misunderstood.

I remember almost
everyday of my life —
childhood rugby,
a near fatal traffic accident.
At thirty-one began
thoughts of future senility.

I wouldn't trade adventures
for mediocre memories.
If my destiny is to fall apart
I shall give away limbs
after using them to print text
hidden under pillows
by those who say my name in vain.

I'll leave more than I took.

Loss

On the subway a woman barks like a dog, her husband holds her hand. The man of professorial stature mumbles nothings into ears while in line at the fast-food restaurant. Without provocation an employee gives his boss details: why he must see a dentist, her looks, an exact address.

Conspiracy theory TV is primetime fodder.

Some say it's Armageddon, point to Mayan calendars which they cannot read. Claim to be archaeologists; experts of ancient documents with online degrees.

Others blame political incompetence.

"Is everyone losing their minds?"

"Don't worry. It's not you."

Epitaph 5

Dead Language

Duke said the term jazz died 'round '43.
Other words/terms we use that no longer exist:

Fairplay
truth
journalism
hip-hop
freedom
evil
gentleman
lady
humility
Dodo bird
Latin.

Love?

No, love still exists.

Timbre

I

We can still hear the reverberation —
timbre from stolen drums.

They once gave this place a pulse
louder than the clang of industry.
We've become fat fencing them,
that's why anorexic bulimia
is fashionable.
Why our bodies' image
screams, "Give what we have gained
back to the Earth."

Drum echoes still ring.

This is how guilt feels.
A thief who never robbed a bank —
never shop-lifted.
Purging —
pushing the feeling away
but the song of drums
still kisses the air.

II

What an odd couple.

Sexually, a neon-light lady bends.
Her neighbour, a plastic good Samaritan,
reaches downward in the opposite direction —
a strip club and church share walls naturally.

Both are welcoming —
signs from above
looking down on pedestrians,
yet their eyes never meet.

III

He wore his jock strap as a face mask —
I thought this was funny.
Swallowed a chest full of laughter.
Our subway car was silent —
afraid to ingest the air.

Epitaph 13

Death Bed

As one gets older, it's said that your singing voice goes flat.
Yours was not, young sharp vocals now pitch perfect.
Days filled singing compositions to Joni, and a tape recorder.
Nights surrounded by your litter of children, ex-wives —
all a myriad of skin tones. Race washed away.
Love of your failing form the only commonality.

This will be your last time in New York,
your last trip to Mexico,
soon the music will stop.

The three of you will finally rest.

Egg Drop and Mushroom Soup

Surrounded by carbon copy facsimiles, jovial acquaintances and compatriots pass servings of general tao chicken, mushroom fried rice. Couples featuring beautiful, petite, high-pitched pixies and their average looking men chirp around us. Our table is obsessed with the merits of plot driven pornography.

"This egg drop soup is delicious."

My mind wonders to the theory that teleportation involves dying in one place, being simultaneously recreated in another.

"Wow, these plastic chopsticks are horrible."

Their shelf lives staggered in similar homes, in similar neighbourhoods with similar offspring mourning in a similar fashion upon their passing.

"I ordered the seafood chow mein but I can't eat it all — I'm allergic to shellfish."

These late-night daydreams are the manifestation of a brainwashed society collapsing. The only unique people in the restaurant sit at a table featuring ill-mannered poets — at least the wait staff wear uniforms.

"She just taught me how to read tea leaves. Yours tell me that your going to successfully jump hurdles and yours say that you should grow a garden."

If I could die in one place and be simultaneously reborn in another place, and be the exact same age, where would I want to die and where would I wish to be reborn?

I would die here, now.

I would die at Bay and Bloor

I would die with my ex-wife pointing and laughing

I would die after a long kiss from you

I would be reborn eating shawarma somewhere on St. Laurent
in Montreal

I would be reborn buying old records on Haight

I would be reborn on the family farm in Jamaica

I would be reborn in Warwick Park, Bermuda

I would be reborn arms wrapped around you blessing the day
scientists figured out teleportation.

"Excuse me, can we have our bill please?"

I would pray that in my new life I had a job that would allow me
to buy you a ticket where I was reassembled. My identical twin
and I have less in common than the couples in this restaurant
have in common. How is that?

"No we don't need change."

When did society decide that passivity and B-movie acting
would replace romance? Thank god you and I missed the email,
maybe we should check our junk box.

"Can you pack these to go?"

"I'm running late. But I'll be by your side in a few seconds."

"Thanks, have a good night."

"I'm home."

"No, I just got here."

Time Travellers

Who are the loneliest people in the world?
My guess: Time travellers
When love fails it's off to the machine
Time to rewrite affairs;
avoid heartache.

The time traveller never truly
invests in love.
He thinks he can figure her out this time.
She believes she can make him feel this time.

Physical touch is a question mark
the time traveller wrestles with.
If the moment is true,
were other moments false?
When physics and metaphysics collide.

The loneliest people in the world
manipulate history,
question imagination,
wandering aimlessly
as forgotten images of the past.

The Cedar Tree

When these eyelids connect for the final time, this mind shall dream itself into a cedar tree. Be home to generations of critters who live peacefully in a silent forest until they witness me crashing to the earth.

All trees fall down.

To know me is to know the big ol' tree I call mentor. A man who could draw better than Picasso. As a child he was as gifted as Pablo, but as an adult he scared me straight: taking my brother and I to his apartment so that we could witness how a drug addict lives.

To him we were mirrors. Saplings who didn't quite fit in and he already memorized the path we were taking, replanting my roots in the earth he uprooted from. But all trees fall down.

Robbed an unlucky old lady, with the wrong set of friends. No, you witnessed a partner in crime murder her, and today I wonder how a man who loved his mother could let a woman old enough to be his mother get killed. It was probably the drugs.

And all trees fall down.

As I became an adult you became a prisoner. No one told you that super heroes aren't allowed to fall like autumn leaves — leaving us. You fell down the steps of recovery. I felt like I hit every branch on the way down. Placed pen to paper; attempted to paint landscapes in the minds of those who began to believe in me. But I can't draw like Picasso. Could never quit art school and become a drug dealer, get deported selling drugs to kids, then save children from themselves.

I want to be a tree. Shade children from rain, birds from storms; be a nesting place for squirrels. Become a place called home; a community.

I'm a failure — fall for termites who threaten my roots until great storms wash them away. Sometimes I forget what the big ol' tree taught me. Realize I'm not built for drama. Forced to reassess everything that is me. When I look up, I realize that my canopy has expanded again. My roots reach deeper into the earth. Someone helped me build a good foundation.

It's been nearly 20 years. Hopefully you're out on probation. If I ever have wealth I shall share it with you. Even great trees fall down. Even trees blown on their sides from stormy weather grow towards the shining sun. The birds don't fly away; they adapt. Become the majestic living arbour you dreamt to be when you first placed brush to canvas as a child. If you're still breathing, there's still time to grow even if you do fall down.

We met when you were the age I am now. I look 20 years younger than you did. I've become the struggling artist that you wanted to be. If we cross paths I will tell you what could have been. The places you should have seen with your own eyes: the cities, the women. But be forewarned, from this point on, I shall grow beyond your personal fantasies.

And when these tired eyelids connect for the final time, this mind shall dream itself into a cedar tree. I shall be home to generations of creatures who live peacefully in a silent forest. One day I will look at the life dependent on my existence. Notice how close the sun feels from such great heights. Smile with the knowledge that I became what I always wanted.

If I'm lucky, this simple cedar shall inspire a child who can draw better than Picasso. Growing to the size of a wild rubber tree: ever expanding. Become the forest itself. And when I fall, I shall block the path that you chose. The earth will be kissed with the aroma of a magnificent cedar. I shall become one with mother nature.

Energy can not die, it can only change form. So when I pass away, I shall be reborn ...

Epitaph 14

Dizzy called you a great administrator.
I never knew a secretary could look so ugly,
or sound so sweet in quadraphonic sound.

Notes

The terms "wildstyle," and "tag" in "How Great Thou Art" are graffiti terms.

"Resuscitation" mentions W. Somerset Maugham's novel, *The Razor's Edge*, and references Ottawa based documentary film-maker, and poet Garmamie Sideau.

Segment II of "A Silent Revolution" centres around the ritualistic behaviour of Guy Fawkes Day in rural Commonwealth communities. Part i of segment II mentions slavery abolitionist William Wilberforce. Part ii references the film, *The Warriors*, directed by Walter Hill.

The term "wining" (wine-ing) in "Dancehall" is a type of dance that features couples grinding their bodies in a rhythmic pattern.

The term "fencing" in the poem "timbre" refers to the informal meaning of the word — to sell stolen goods.

The quote, "Parting is such sweet sorrow," featured in the poem "The Castle" is originally from Shakespeare's *Romeo and Juliet*.

Anglhost — a word created for "If Roles Were Reversed" — is the combination of ghost, and Anglo-Saxon.

The term "pen" in "Fear — a work in two voices" refers to a female swan.

The Epitaph poems are influenced by the following Charles Mingus recordings, film, and books:

The Complete City Hall Recording

At UCLA, 1965

Let the Children Hear Music

Pre-Bird

Triumph of the Underdog directed by Don McGlynn

Mingus/Mingus: Two Views, Janet Coleman, and Al Young, Berkeley: Creative Arts Book Company, 1989

Mingus: A Critical Biography, Brian Priestly, London: Quartet Books, 1982

Tonight at Noon: A Love Story, Sue Mingus, LA: Pantheon, 2002

Beneath the Underdog, Charles Mingus, NY: Vintage, 1971

Acknowledgements

I would like to thank the publishers of *Chrysalis Zine, Burner Magazine, 2013 Big Art Book, Numero Cinq, Variations Magazine, Papirmass, Rise Ashen's Earth Dragon LP*, and the *Paris Collective* for featuring earlier versions of poems in this collection.

I would also like to acknowledge the Ontario Arts Council, and Guernica Editions for supporting my research through a Writer's Reserve Grant.

Additionally, I would like to recognize the support of Dan D'Onorio, Anna Saini, Pat Connors, Mike Lipsius, Nicci and my direct family — Malcolm, Yvette, Malcolm Brian and Dene Stanley.

About the Author

With a publishing history that spans four nations, the writings of Dane Swan include: poetry, prose, and editorials on literature and popular culture. Bermuda born, with Jamaican heritage, Dane is based in Toronto, Canada. A former Writer In Residence for Open Book Toronto, he has also been short-listed for the Monica Ladell Award. Swan's work has been taught in schools and featured in print, online, on vinyl and CD. His first collection of poetry, *Bending The Continuum*, was published by Guernica Editions.

MARQUIS

Québec, Canada

RECYCLED
Paper made from
recycled material
FSC® C103567

Printed on Enviro 100% post-consumer EcoLogo certified paper,
processed chlorine free and manufactured using biogas energy.

100%

PERMANENT